Alfred's Premier Piano Course

Carol Matz • Victoria McArthur

Contents

Metronome: © Shutterstock.com / fishandfish

Glasses isolated: © istockphoto.com / GlobalStock

Copyright © 2014 by Alfred Music

All Rights Reserved. Printed in USA.

ISBN-10: 0-7390-9633-8

ISBN-13: 978-0-7390-9633-8

A Note to Teachers

Why Sight-Read?

- Sight-reading has been described by many pianists as being their most cherished, practical, and long-lasting skill gleaned from piano study.

- Good sight-readers are more motivated pianists since the often-tedious phase of slow note-reading is minimized, leading to a "finished" version of a piece more quickly.

- Good sight-readers are able to participate in ensembles, accompany choirs and dancers, or play for other special events.

How to Use the Sight-Reading Book

Sight-Reading 1B is divided into 14 units. Each unit contains five short activities. The pages in each unit are correlated page by page with the material in *Lesson Book 1B*. They should be assigned according to the instructions in the upper-right corner of each page of this book.

- You may assign the student to do one activity per day, with all activities in a unit being completed in a five-day cycle.

- The student *should not* practice the activity but instead should do it only once (with the repeat).

- Some students will be able to complete more than one activity per day.

- You may want to hear selected activities at the lesson to check the student's progress.

What Are the Five Activities?

Activity 1

Play the Note: Students will play individual notes using finger 2 to break down any reliance on playing in set positions. The first few exercises in this book begin with a review of the notes learned in *Level 1A*. New Landmark Notes are gradually introduced in *Level 1B*. Students gradually play notes further away from the Landmarks in later exercises. The goal is to recognize and play note patterns without relying on the previous note as a reference. This is similar to note identification with flashcards.

Activity 2

Play from Note-to-Note: Students play patterns with intervals of 2nds (steps), 3rds (skips), 4ths, and 5ths from Landmark Notes. The goal is to recognize and play note patterns using the previous note as a reference.

Activity 3

Rhythm Challenge: Students tap rhythm patterns on either the closed keyboard cover or on their laps. The goal is to perform rhythm patterns accurately while keeping a steady beat.

Activity 4

Play Without Stopping: Students play a short piece that uses the *Rhythm Challenge* patterns. The goal is to keep playing without pause. Some students may wish to play with a metronome as an additional challenge.

Activity 5

Play Expressively: Students play a short variation of the *Play Without Stopping* piece. Dynamic and tempo indications are stressed in this piece. The goal is to play expressively without stopping.

A Note to Students

Learning to sight-read at the piano
is exciting and important!

Why?

- Sight-reading is different from
  practicing since you often have only
  one chance to play each piece as you
  try to do your best the first time.

- As you learn to sight-read well, all
  your music sounds better more quickly!
  You will have more time to play *more*
  music you enjoy with your extra time!

- You can play music on your own
  for fun, along with others as a duet
  partner, or as an accompanist.

How this book will help you become a Premier Sight-Reader

Your teacher will suggest ways to do the activities in this book. You can
make a check-mark or draw a star in the box next to the activity when
you have completed it.

Activity 1
Play the Note: Write the names of the notes in
the boxes, then play each note with finger 2 only.

Activity 2
Play from Note-to-Note: Write the names of the
notes in the boxes, then play. Notice whether notes
move up, down, or stay the same. Also notice the
interval (2nd, 3rd, 4th, or 5th) between each note.

Activity 3
Rhythm Challenge: Tap the rhythm on the closed
keyboard cover or on your lap. Count and keep a
steady beat.

Activity 4
Play Without Stopping: Choose a tempo at
which you can play with a steady beat. Keep going,
even if you play a wrong note or must skip some
notes. For an additional challenge, play this activity
with a metronome.

Activity 5
Play Expressively: Circle all tempo and dynamic
markings. Then play, as you make your music
sound as expressive as you can. Your playing will be
more interesting if you use the expression marks.

Unit 1: Review

☐ Activity 1 Play the Note

Write the names of the notes in the boxes. Then, play each note using finger 2.

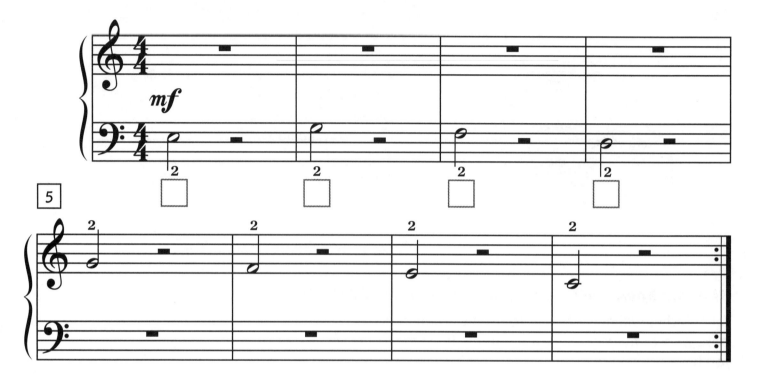

☐ Activity 2 Play from Note-to-Note

Write the names of the notes in the boxes, then play.

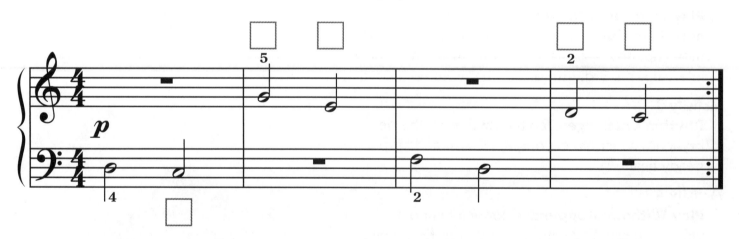

☐ Activity 3 Rhythm Challenge

Tap the rhythm on the closed keyboard cover or on your lap.
Count and keep a steady beat.

☐ Activity 4 **Play Without Stopping**

Choose a tempo at which you can play with a steady beat.
Keep going, even if you play a wrong note or leave notes out.
Challenge: Play with a metronome (♩ = 112–126).

Toy Rocket

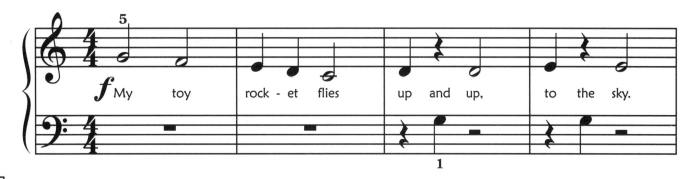

My toy rock-et flies up and up, to the sky.

Did not know it could get up that high!

☐ Activity 5 **Play Expressively**

Circle all the tempo and dynamic markings.
Then play, making the music as expressive as you can.

Paper Airplanes

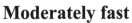

Moderately fast

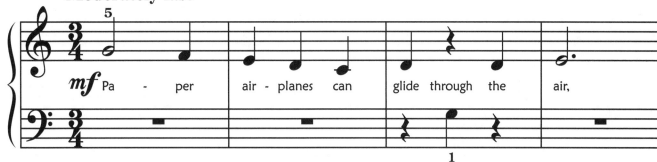

Pa - per air-planes can glide through the air,

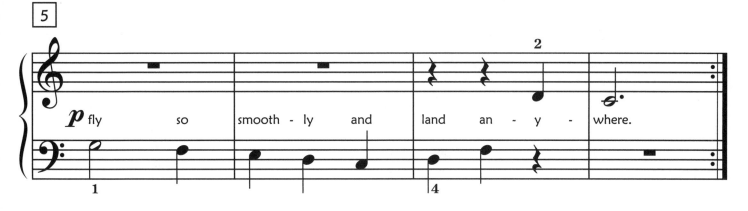

fly so smooth-ly and land an-y-where.

6

Unit 2: C 5-Finger Pattern

☐ Activity 1 Play the Note

Write the names of the notes in the boxes. Then, play each note using finger 2.

☐ Activity 2 Play from Note-to-Note

Write the names of the notes in the boxes, then play.

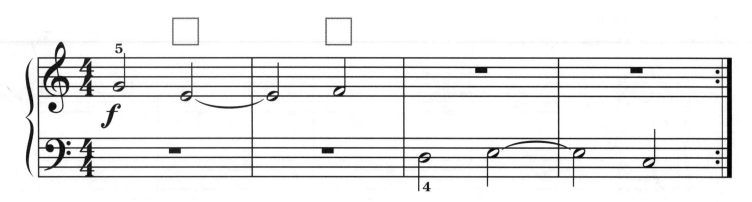

☐ Activity 3 Rhythm Challenge

Tap the rhythm on the closed keyboard cover or on your lap.
Count and keep a steady beat.

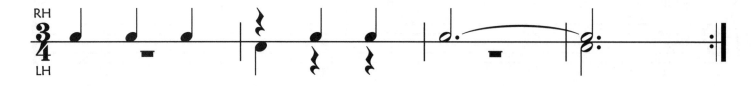

❏ Activity 4 Play Without Stopping

Choose a tempo at which you can play with a steady beat.
Keep going, even if you play a wrong note or leave notes out.
Challenge: Play with a metronome (♩ = 100–120).

Picnic in the Park

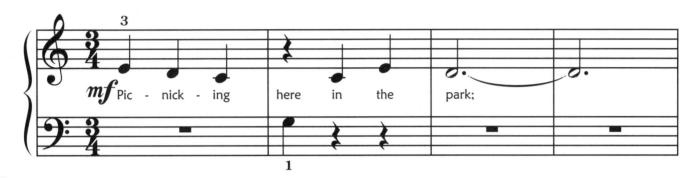

❏ Activity 5 Play Expressively

Circle all the tempo and dynamic markings.
Then play, making the music as expressive as you can.

Our Barbecue

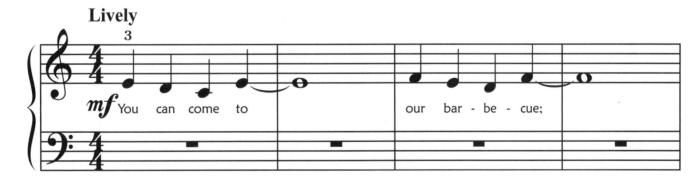

8

Unit 3: New Note A

☐ Activity 1 Play the Note

Write the names of the notes in the boxes. Then, play each note using finger 2.

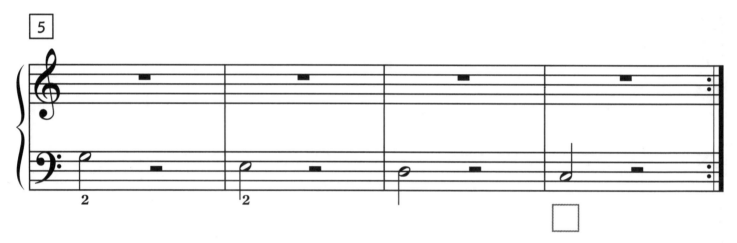

☐ Activity 2 Play from Note-to-Note

Write the names of the notes in the boxes, then play.

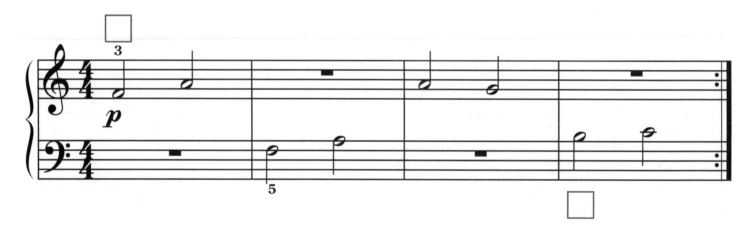

☐ Activity 3 Rhythm Challenge

Tap the rhythm on the closed keyboard cover or on your lap.
Count and keep a steady beat.

☐ Activity 4 Play Without Stopping

Choose a tempo at which you can play with a steady beat.
Keep going, even if you play a wrong note or leave notes out.
Challenge: Play with a metronome (♩ = 100–120).

Chinese Lanterns

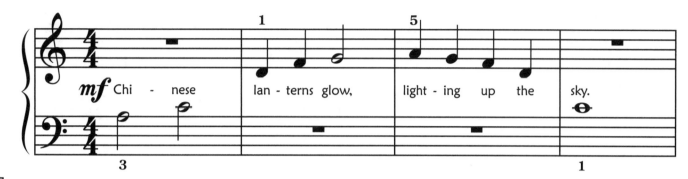

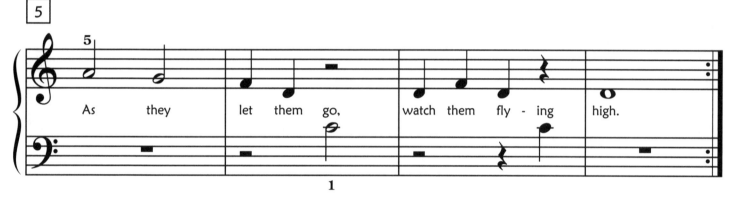

☐ Activity 5 Play Expressively

Circle all the tempo and dynamic markings.
Then play, making the music as expressive as you can.

Chinese Festival

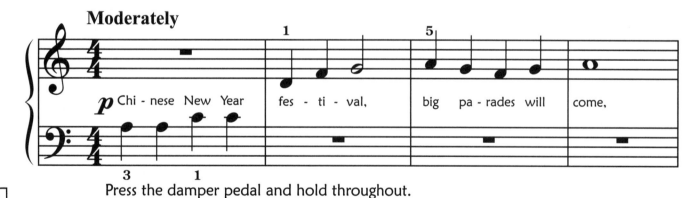

Press the damper pedal and hold throughout.

Unit 4: Legato and Staccato

❏ Activity 1 **Play the Note**

Write the names of the notes in the boxes. Then, play each note using finger 2.

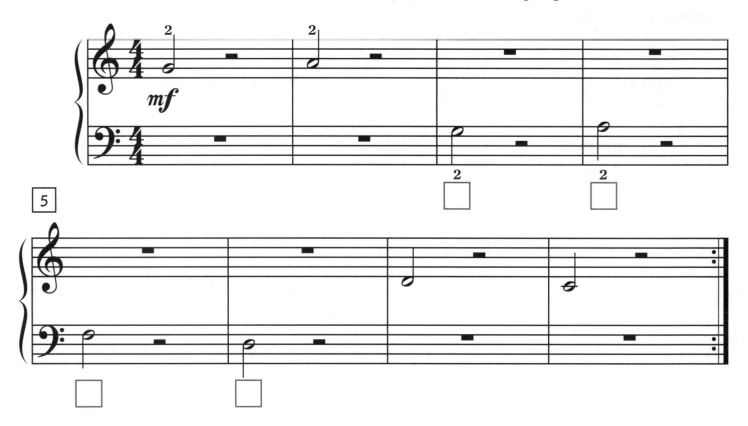

❏ Activity 2 **Play from Note-to-Note**

Write the names of the notes in the boxes, then play.

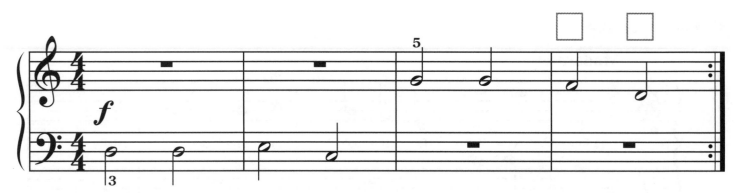

❏ Activity 3 **Rhythm Challenge**

Tap the rhythm on the closed keyboard cover or on your lap.
Count and keep a steady beat.

❏ Activity 4 Play Without Stopping

Choose a tempo at which you can play with a steady beat.
Keep going, even if you play a wrong note or leave notes out.
Challenge: Play with a metronome (♩ = 112–126).

Bounce the Basketball

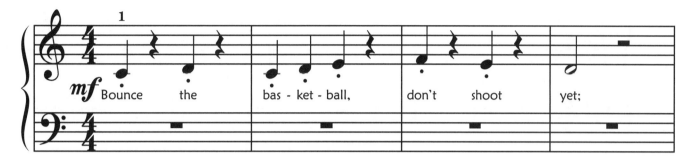

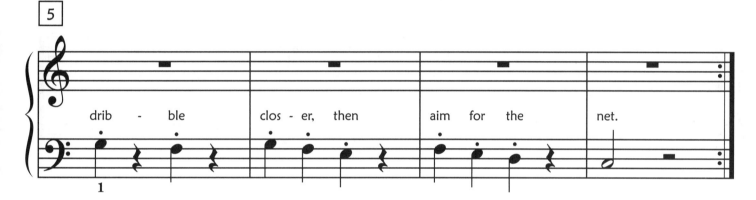

❏ Activity 5 Play Expressively

Circle all the tempo and dynamic markings.
Then play, making the music as expressive as you can.

Bowling

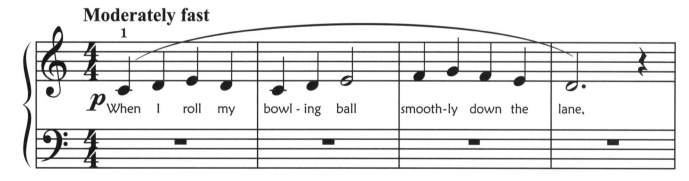

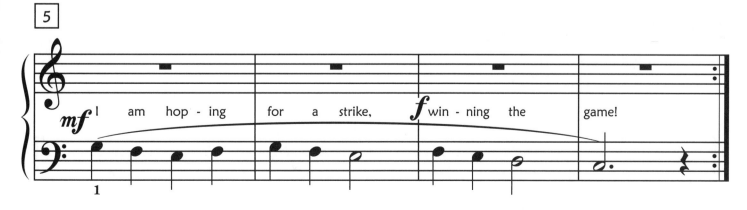

Lesson Book: page 17

Unit 5: New Rhythm (𝄴 ♩ 𝄽 ♩ 𝄽 | ♩ 𝄽 – ‖)

❑ Activity 1 Play the Note

Write the names of the notes in the boxes. Then, play each note using finger 2.

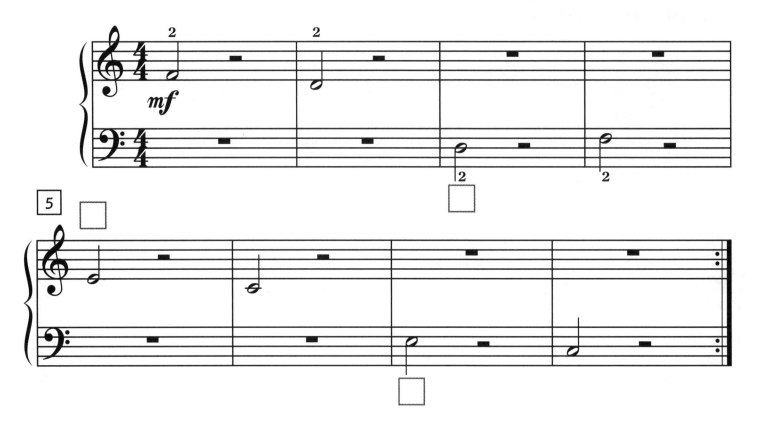

❑ Activity 2 Play from Note-to-Note

Write the names of the notes in the boxes, then play.

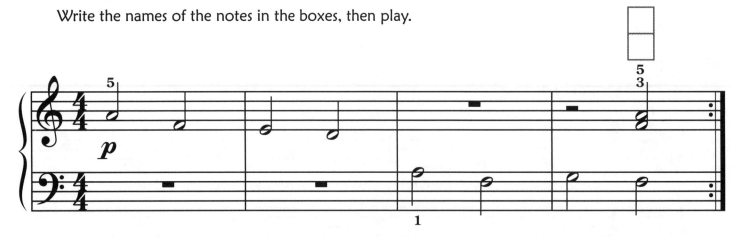

❑ Activity 3 Rhythm Challenge

Tap the rhythm on the closed keyboard cover or on your lap.
Count and keep a steady beat.

❑ Activity 4 Play Without Stopping

Choose a tempo at which you can play with a steady beat.
Keep going, even if you play a wrong note or leave notes out.
Challenge: Play with a metronome (♩ = 112–126).

Australian Kangaroo

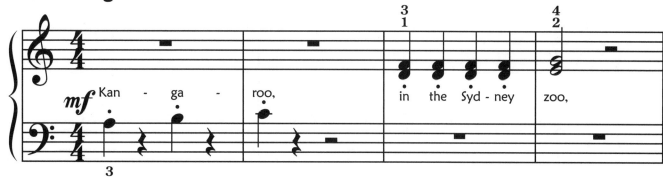

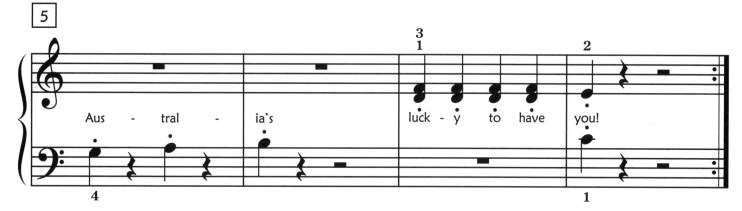

❑ Activity 5 Play Expressively

Circle all the tempo and dynamic markings.
Then play, making the music as expressive as you can.

Slithering Python

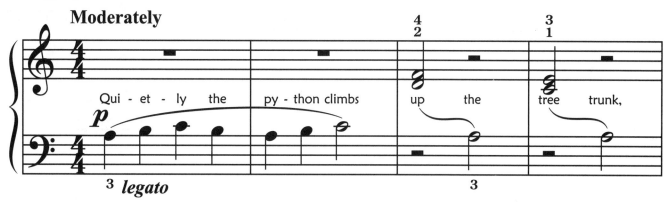

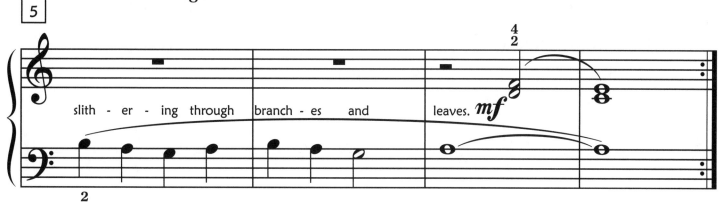

14

Unit 6: 2nds and 3rds

❏ Activity 1 **Play the Note**

Write the names of the notes in the boxes. Then, play each note using finger 2.

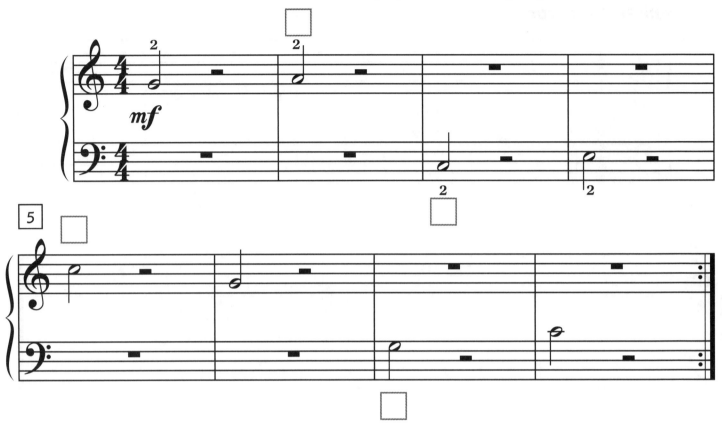

❏ Activity 2 **Play from Note-to-Note**

Write the names of the notes in the boxes, then play.

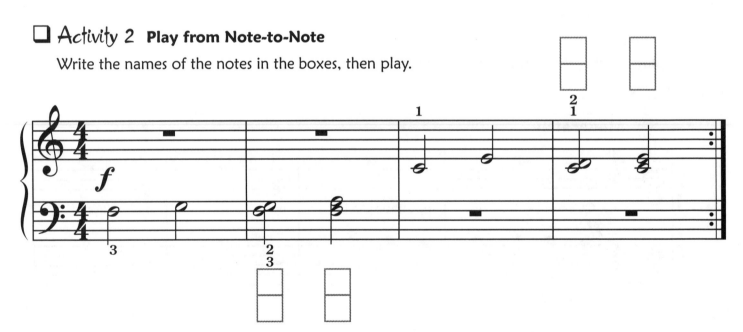

❏ Activity 3 **Rhythm Challenge**

Tap the rhythm on the closed keyboard cover or on your lap.
Count and keep a steady beat.

❑ Activity 4 Play Without Stopping

Choose a tempo at which you can play with a steady beat.
Keep going, even if you play a wrong note or leave notes out.
Challenge: Play with a metronome (♩ = 100–120).

Carnival Carousel

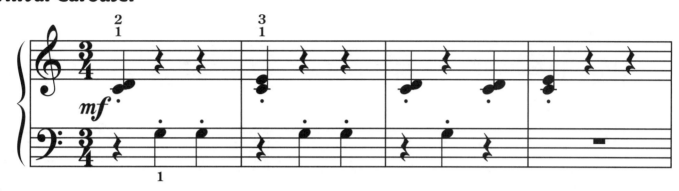

❑ Activity 5 Play Expressively

Circle all the tempo and dynamic markings.
Then play, making the music as expressive as you can.

The Fun House

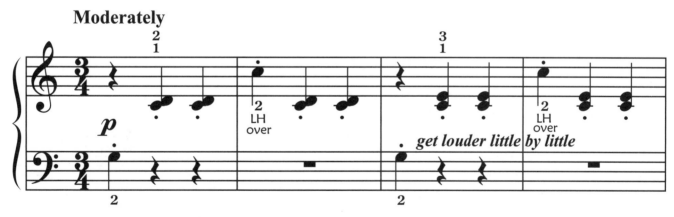

Unit 7: G 5-Finger Pattern for RH

☐ Activity 1 Play the Note

Write the names of the notes in the boxes. Then, play each note using finger 2.

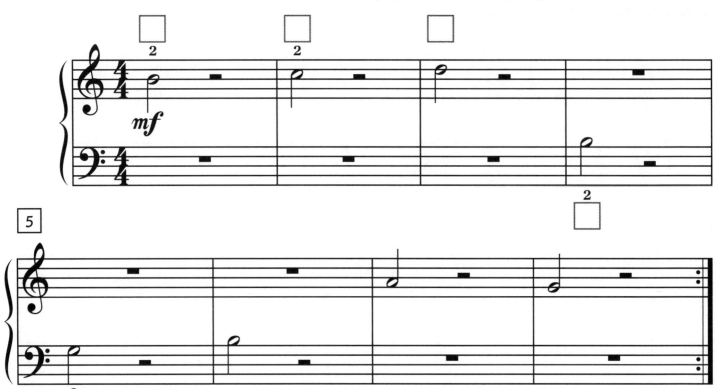

☐ Activity 2 Play from Note-to-Note

Write the names of the notes in the boxes, then play.

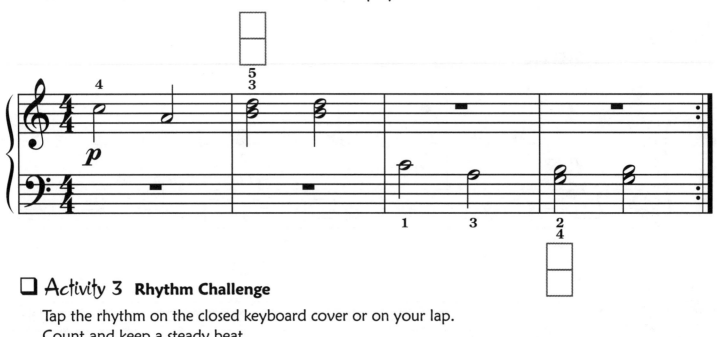

☐ Activity 3 Rhythm Challenge

Tap the rhythm on the closed keyboard cover or on your lap.
Count and keep a steady beat.

❑ Activity 4 Play Without Stopping

Choose a tempo at which you can play with a steady beat.
Keep going, even if you play a wrong note or leave notes out.
Challenge: Play with a metronome (♩ = 100–120).

Playing Tag

We're play - ing   tag,   we nev - er   quit.

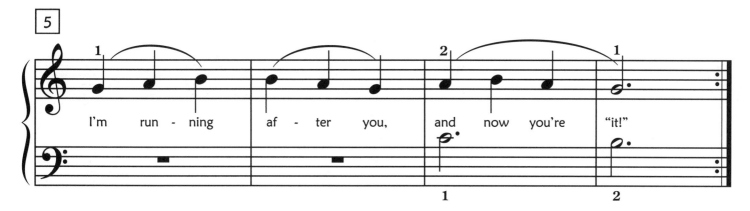

I'm run - ning   af - ter   you,   and   now   you're   "it!"

❑ Activity 5 Play Expressively

Circle all the tempo and dynamic markings.
Then play, making the music as expressive as you can.

Playing Hide and Seek

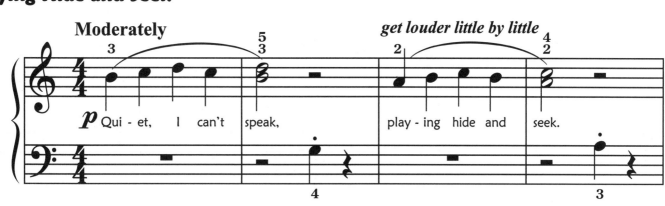

Qui - et,   I   can't   speak,   play - ing   hide   and   seek.

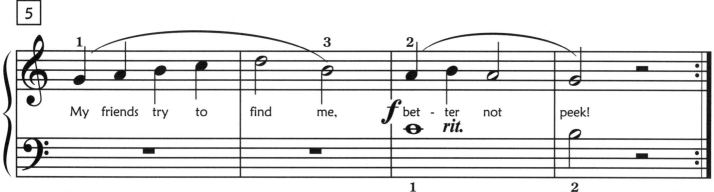

My   friends   try   to   find   me,   *f* bet - ter   not   *rit.*   peek!

Unit 8: G 5-Finger Pattern for LH

☐ Activity 1 **Play the Note**

Write the names of the notes in the boxes. Then, play each note using finger 2.

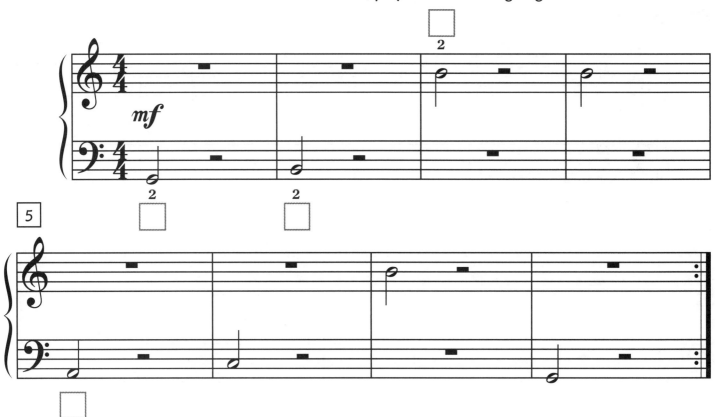

☐ Activity 2 **Play from Note-to-Note**

Write the names of the notes in the boxes, then play.

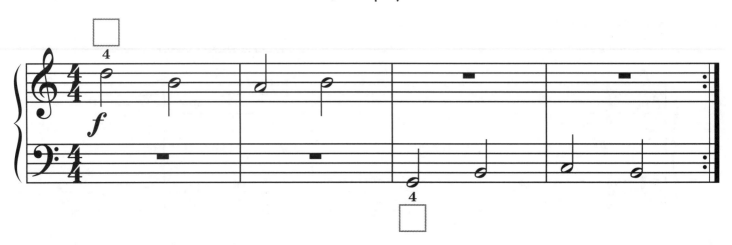

☐ Activity 3 **Rhythm Challenge**

Tap the rhythm on the closed keyboard cover or on your lap.
Count and keep a steady beat.

❏ Activity 4 Play Without Stopping

Choose a tempo at which you can play with a steady beat.
Keep going, even if you play a wrong note or leave notes out.
Challenge: Play with a metronome (♩ = 100–120).

The Cello's Song

❏ Activity 5 Play Expressively

Circle all the tempo and dynamic markings.
Then play, making the music as expressive as you can.

Marching Trombones

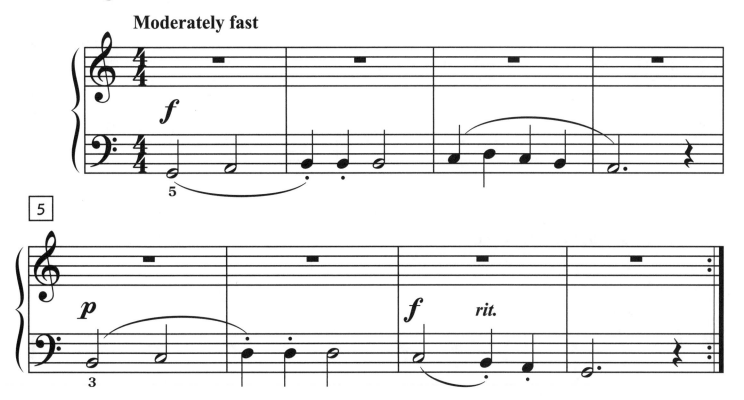

Lesson Book: page 31

Unit 9: 4ths

☐ Activity 1 Play the Note

Write the names of the notes in the boxes. Then, play each note using finger 2.

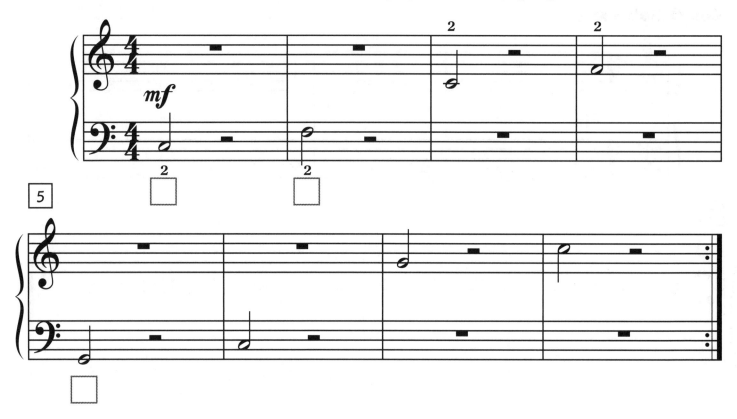

☐ Activity 2 Play from Note-to-Note

Write the names of the notes in the boxes, then play.

☐ Activity 3 Rhythm Challenge

Tap the rhythm on the closed keyboard cover or on your lap.
Count and keep a steady beat.

❑ Activity 4 **Play Without Stopping**

Choose a tempo at which you can play with a steady beat.
Keep going, even if you play a wrong note or leave notes out.
Challenge: Play with a metronome (♩ = 100–120).

Circus Juggler

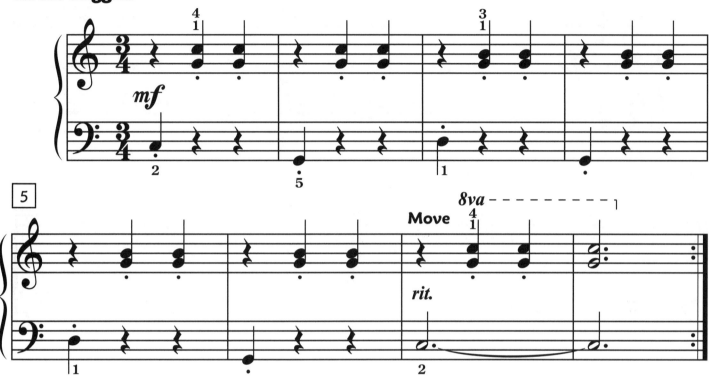

❑ Activity 5 **Play Expressively**

Circle all the tempo and dynamic markings.
Then play, making the music as expressive as you can.

Flying Trapeze

Unit 10: 5ths

☐ Activity 1 Play the Note

Write the names of the notes in the boxes. Then, play each note using finger 2.

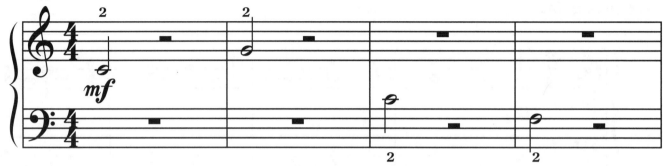

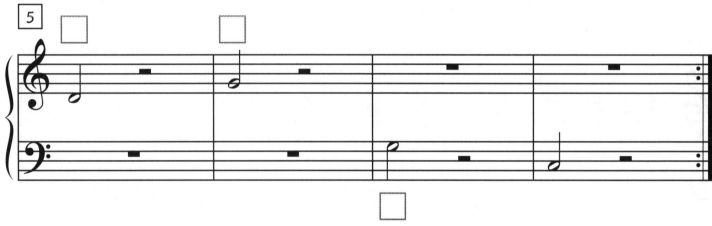

☐ Activity 2 Play from Note-to-Note

Write the names of the notes in the boxes, then play.

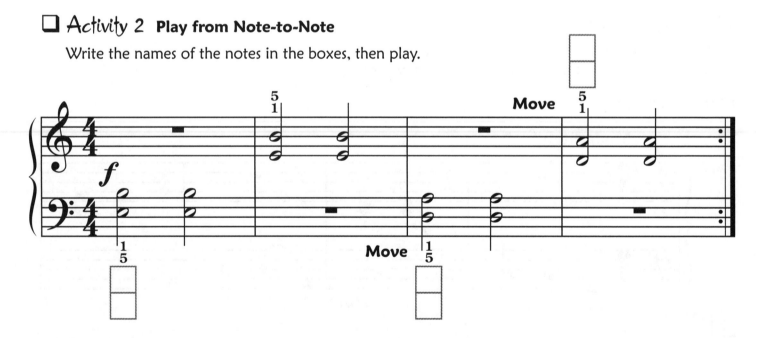

☐ Activity 3 Rhythm Challenge

Tap the rhythm on the closed keyboard cover or on your lap.
Count and keep a steady beat.

❏ Activity 4 Play Without Stopping

Choose a tempo at which you can play with a steady beat.
Keep going, even if you play a wrong note or leave notes out.
Challenge: Play with a metronome (♩ = 100–120).

Falling Leaves

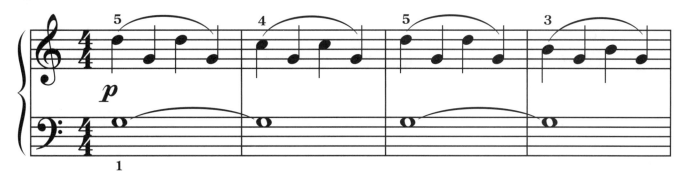

Press the damper pedal and hold throughout.

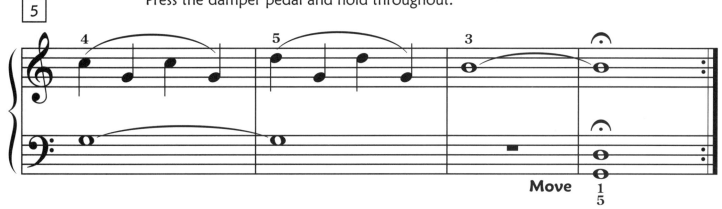

Move

❏ Activity 5 Play Expressively

Circle all the tempo and dynamic markings.
Then play, making the music as expressive as you can.

Winter Winds

Press the damper pedal and hold throughout.

Move

24

Unit 11: Sharps

❏ Activity 1 **Play the Note**

Write the names of the notes in the boxes. Then, play each note using finger 2.

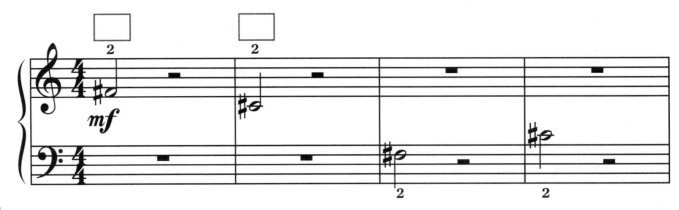

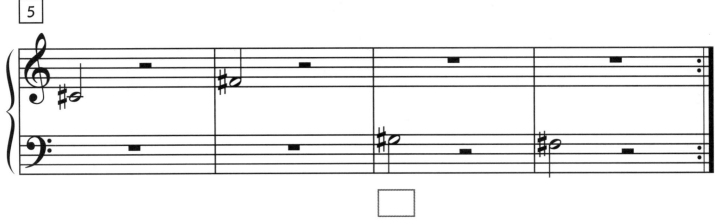

❏ Activity 2 **Play from Note-to-Note**

Write the names of the notes in the boxes, then play.

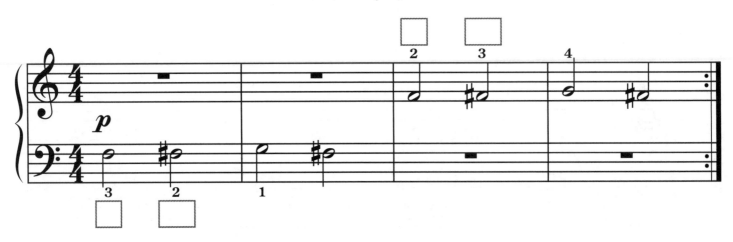

❏ Activity 3 **Rhythm Challenge**

Tap the rhythm on the closed keyboard cover or on your lap.
Count and keep a steady beat.

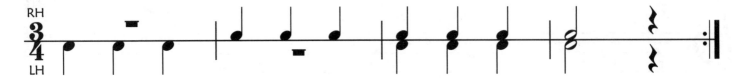

❏ Activity 4 Play Without Stopping

Choose a tempo at which you can play with a steady beat.
Keep going, even if you play a wrong note or leave notes out.
Challenge: Play with a metronome (♩ = 100–120).

My Scooter

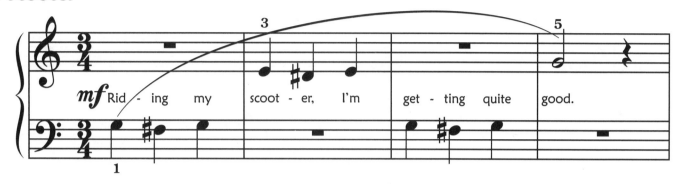

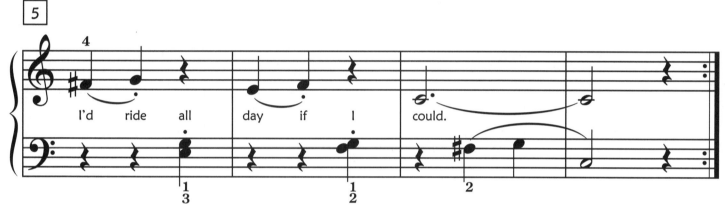

❏ Activity 5 Play Expressively

Circle all the tempo and dynamic markings.
Then play, making the music as expressive as you can.

My New Soccer Ball

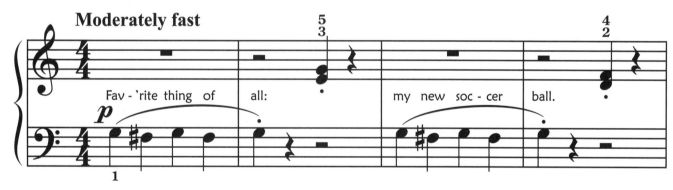

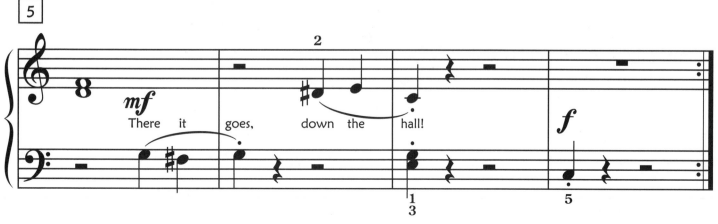

Lesson Book: page 39

Unit 12: New Note D

☐ Activity 1 **Play the Note**

Write the names of the notes in the boxes. Then, play each note using finger 2.

☐ Activity 2 **Play from Note-to-Note**

Write the names of the notes in the boxes, then play.

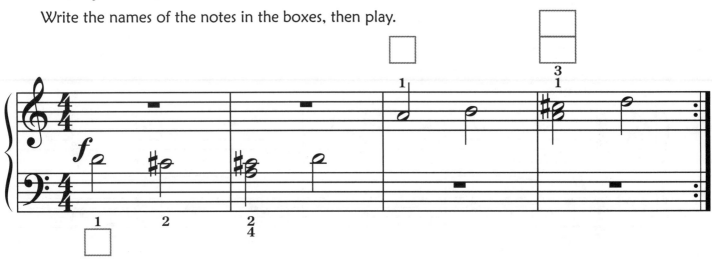

☐ Activity 3 **Rhythm Challenge**

Tap the rhythm on the closed keyboard cover or on your lap.
Count and keep a steady beat.

☐ Activity 4 Play Without Stopping

Choose a tempo at which you can play with a steady beat.
Keep going, even if you play a wrong note or leave notes out.
Challenge: Play with a metronome (♩ = 100–120).

The Birthday Present

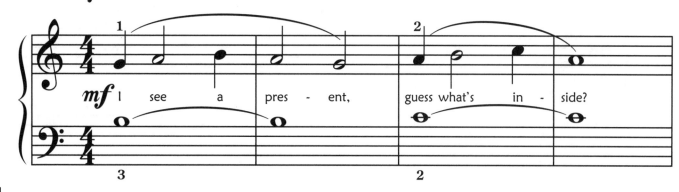

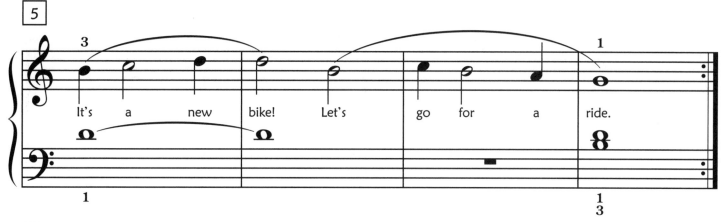

☐ Activity 5 Play Expressively

Circle all the tempo and dynamic markings.
Then play, making the music as expressive as you can.

My Birthday

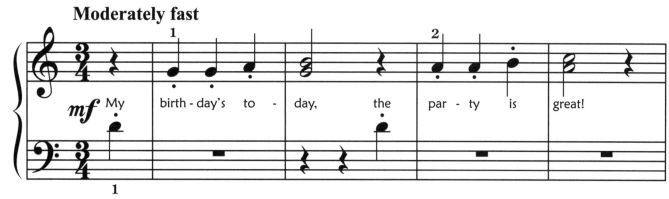

Unit 13: Flats

❑ Activity 1 **Play the Note**

Write the names of the notes in the boxes. Then, play each note using finger 2.

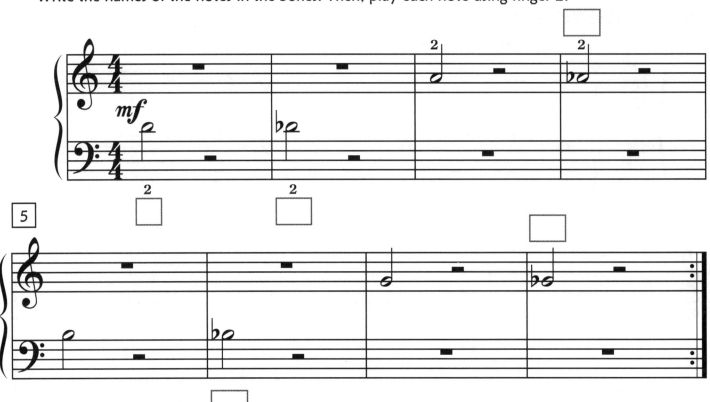

❑ Activity 2 **Play from Note-to-Note**

Write the names of the notes in the boxes, then play.

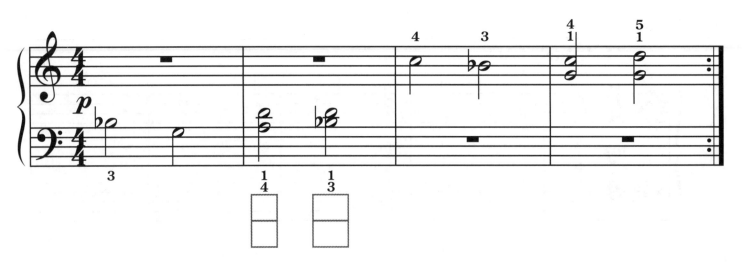

❑ Activity 3 **Rhythm Challenge**

Tap the rhythm on the closed keyboard cover or on your lap.
Count and keep a steady beat.

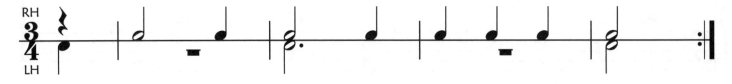

☐ Activity 4 Play Without Stopping

Choose a tempo at which you can play with a steady beat.
Keep going, even if you play a wrong note or leave notes out.
Challenge: Play with a metronome (♩ = 92–112).

The Tadpole

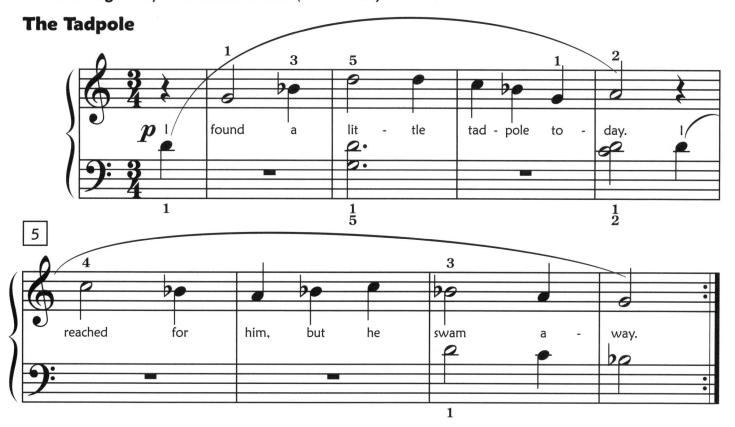

☐ Activity 5 Play Expressively

Circle all the tempo and dynamic markings.
Then play, making the music as expressive as you can.

The Frog

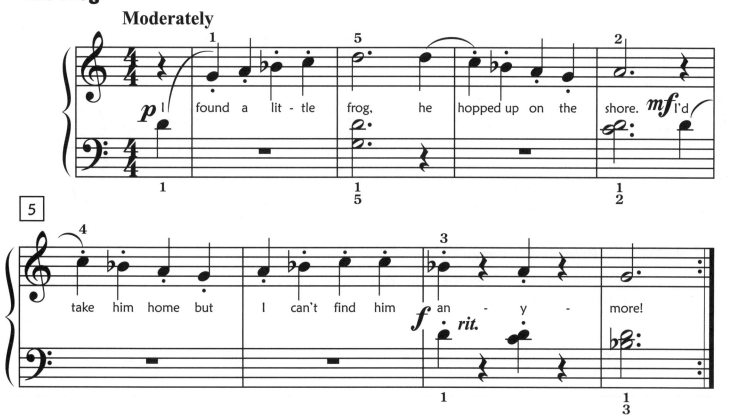

Unit 14: Review

❑ Activity 1 Play the Note

Write the names of the notes in the boxes. Then, play each note using finger 2.

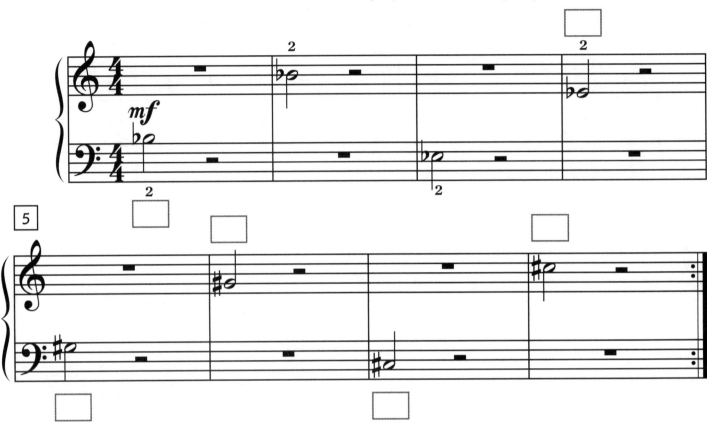

❑ Activity 2 Play from Note-to-Note

Write the names of the notes in the boxes, then play.

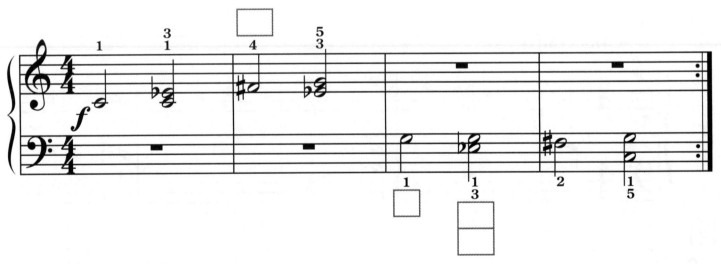

❑ Activity 3 Rhythm Challenge

Tap the rhythm on the closed keyboard cover or on your lap.
Count and keep a steady beat.

❑ Activity 4 Play Without Stopping

Choose a tempo at which you can play with a steady beat.
Keep going, even if you play a wrong note or leave notes out.
Challenge: Play with a metronome (♩ = 100–120).

Scary Movies

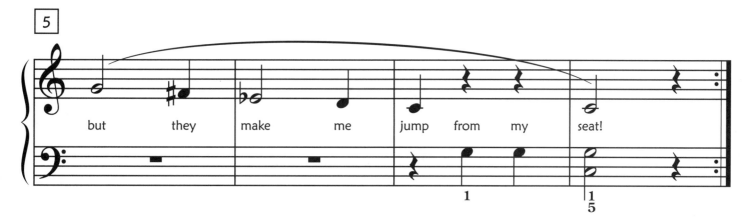

❑ Activity 5 Play Expressively

Circle all the tempo and dynamic markings.
Then play, making the music as expressive as you can.

Scary Dreams

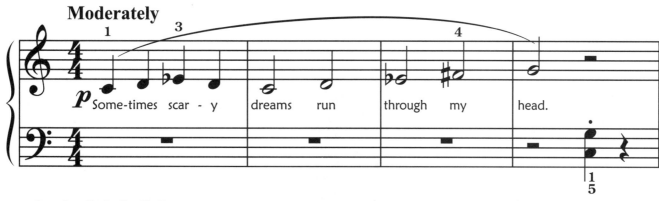

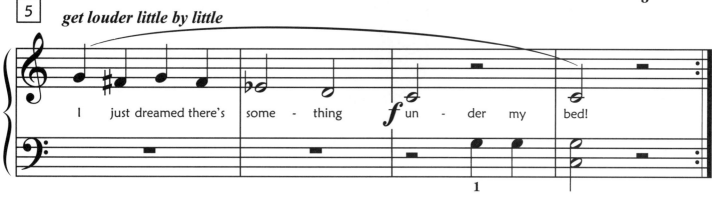

Alfred's Premier Sight-Reading Achievement Award

presented to

_____

Student

**You have
successfully completed
Sight-Reading Book 1B
and are
hereby promoted to
Sight-Reading Book 2A.**

_____   _____

Teacher   _Date_